Form L 31

D1645606

Consider the Years

CONSIDER
THE YEARS
1938-1946

by

VIRGINIA GRAHAM

JONATHAN CAPE
THIRTY BEDFORD SQUARE
LONDON

TO

PETER and CELIA

C- 6194494 -7

361867

821/GRA

FIRST PUBLISHED 1946

———————————

PRINTED IN GREAT BRITAIN IN THE CITY OF OXFORD
AT THE ALDEN PRESS
BOUND BY A. W. BAIN & CO. LTD., LONDON

CONTENTS

7

ACKNOWLEDGMENTS

The Author wishes to express her gratitude to the Proprietors of *Punch* for permission to reprint most of the items in this book, and to the Editors of *Truth*, *Design* and *Lilliput* for permission to reprint the remainder

1938

FOX-TROT

Wrapped in a velvet shroud of fog
The bare countryside lies sleeping under its drifting pall.
Come, my beloved friends, my dear companions,
This surely is a perfect night for the ball.
Several leagues away, down impenetrable lanes,
The ancient county town lies huddled beneath invisible stars,
And there, in the gaily gas-lit Corn Exchange,
The local orchestra is playing the opening bars.
We will leave our coats in a striped built-out tent
Where we shall meet some shivering débutantes and their blue-armed
    mothers.
Clutching blank programmes in stiff anxious fingers,
We will join the others.
The room will be garlanded with foxes' brushes,
Their snarling masks will grin reproachfully down on the happy
    dancers,
Whose own masks, grinning back, bob up and down
To dear old Sir Roger and the Lancers.
Through the mist the gay pink coats will come a-whirling,
They will flick us gently as we sit in a dudgeon by the wall,
For of course our men will be talking cheerfully to one another by the
    buffet
Having forgotten we exist at all.
The drummer of the band will be very comical,
There will be a tall shiny-faced girl in raspberry lace looking forlorn,
There will be shrill, bloodthirsty, thrilling hunting noises,
And someone will blow a horn.
A generous spread will be set before us —
Rosy salmon from a silver tin and small beige quails,
While over our bowed heads whistle pellets of bread,

Flicked very humorously by callow males.
We will order the first car at four,
With Johnson sitting severe and grey-lipped in the driver's seat,
And we will creep turbidly home to snatch an hour's repose
Before we set off again for the Meet.

THE WATCH ON THE RHINE

The life of a Rhinemaiden isn't so hot
   As it looks from the back of the stalls;
We do, it is true, get about quite a lot,
   But the view's much the same, and it palls.

Each performance we're cased from the toes to the waist
   In long piscatorial tails,
Then we're launched from the wings on innumerable strings
   Like a school of benevolent whales.

It isn't much fun to be twiddled around,
   Going Sir Thomas knows where,
Suspended at least thirty feet from the ground,
   It is hard to be Naiad-may-care!

We strive with our arms to display all the charms
   Of sirens who lounge upon rocks,
But our legs are congealed and our bosoms concealed
   In the most unprovocative frocks.

It's a bore to be mouthing like moribund cods
   As we're dazedly, dizzily swung,
While beneath us, obscured from the gallery gods,
   The genuine artists give tongue.

It makes us feel sick when we see Alberich
    Through a shimmering eau-de-Rhin curtain,
And a bird's-view of Frica just makes us feel sicker —
    Of that we are perfectly certain.

At the end of the night we're surprised we're alive,
    For, controlled by invisible winches,
We are forced like recalcitrant penguins to dive,
    Avoiding each other by inches.

We are plagued by the thought that our fins may get caught,
    Or our heavenly workings may jam,
Though we don't want to fuss, it's not happy for us
    To be hung like Virginia Ham.

GENERAL KNOWLEDGE

From my earliest youth I have always been told
    To place my reliance on Facts,
So I know just exactly why ice is so cold
    And why wood or elastic contracts.
I know all the gases which float in the air
    And the number of grains in a pound;
I know an isosceles isn't a square
    And the globe isn't really a round.
I could tell you the distance from here to the sky,
    Trigonometry's child's play to me;
I'm aware of the reason why aeroplanes fly,
    And the cubic contents of the sea.
Fourth-dimensional problems I always enjoy,
    I can understand physics. Besides,
I can tell which is silver and which is alloy,
    I know all about dew and the tides.
I can grasp little things like the volume of space
    And the travelling powers of sound
                        BUT
WHY does a polo-match always take place
    On the opposite side of the ground?

NIGHTFALL

I swear to thee, O God of Locomotion,
   Here on my reverently bended knees,
A life of supernatural devotion
   If, just for once, our motor may not freeze!

Grant me this night that I may dip my candle
   So confident in thy omnipotence,
That when I turn to-morrow's steely handle
   A feline purr shall be my recompense.

Surely it hurts your fond parental ears
   To hear your offspring's loud diurnal gasps,
Her choking cough, her screaming tortured gears,
   And intermittent respitory rasps.

Each morning George and I, with 'she' beside us,
   Pray, as we tug and pull and swear and strain,
That thou, Celestial Sparking Plug, may guide us
   To catch for once the early London train.

O thou to whom all little engines turn,
   Do, I beseech thee, also deign to turn 'em,
Lest it become my everyday concern
   To push my husband all the way to Burnham.

NOW THAT YOU LIVE IN THE COUNTRY

Now that you live in the country,
    you will slowly change your ways,
unwittingly you will turn your back
    on your fuggy London days.

Little by little the urge will grow
    to open each window wide,
and the cold, cold air of the country
    will come surging about inside.

As melts the snow in the sunshine
    the blood in your veins will thaw,
and you'll go round turning the heating off
    and opening every door.

The nearer you get to nature,
    the more, it appears, you perspire;
you will throw off your furs during dinner,
    and let out the drawing-room fire.

You'll believe you're the selfsame person,
    but no, as the years unfold
you'll get hotter and hotter and hotter,
    and your visitors colder than cold.

We shall find, with the stealth of a tortoise,
    unheeded, unheard as a mouse,
though you think you've a house in the country,
    the country's crept into your house!

Adieu, mes petites pantoufles fanées,
    Amies depuis tant d'années!
Point de pompoms maintenant, ni de talons,
    Vous n'êtres plus très convenables pour le salon
De Madame. Mais oui, tournez vite le dos,
    Car voici mes souliers nouveaux,
Mais ils n'auront jamais une douceur telle que la votre. Bah!
    Ces autres la!
Mesquines, pauvres, et sans semelles,
    Vous resterez pour moi, les plus belles,
Et il faut être philosophe, petites pantoufles, car hélas!
    Tout casse, tout lasse, tout passe.

SUNKISSED

(To be sung to the tune of 'A Little Grey Home in the West')

There's a little red V on my chest,
An unsightly affair, you'll agree;
   I was caught by the sun
   On the Friday to Mon.
That I spent down at Bexhill-on-Sea.
And to-night when I go to the Ball
I shall wear mother's Indian shawl,
      FOR
   I fear for the charms
   Of my lily-white arms
With a little red V on my chest.

What avail if I'm looking my best?
What's the use if I'm dressed to a T?
   Every nice man escapes
   Geometrical shapes
On the bosoms of partners-to-be—
All my hopes of romance have gone west,
With a bonfire alight in my breast;
      NO,
   I don't stand a chance,
   They won't ask me to dance,
There's a little red V on my chest.

FACING THE MUSIC

We who love music are not pretty.
    Dear me, no!
Though there be cherished in each hidden heart
The selfsame beauties which inspired Mozart,
    Our bodies singularly fail to show
        them. It's a pity.

In concert halls we slump into our places,
    hair awry.
Feeling in perfect sympathy with Brahms,
We yet but manifest the doubtful charms
    of troglodytes. I wonder why
        we have *such* faces!

Nothing matches. We will wear goloshes,
    baggy coats,
strive all in vain to emulate Miss Sitwell
in gowns which should but do not fit a bit well,
    while over us there languorously floats
        the smell of mackintoshes.

We who love music are not pretty.
    And since our souls
Are spun about with sweet melodious notes,
Why have we bulging brows and pendant throats,
    and downy lips and podgy hands and moles?
        It's such a pity!

1939

SOMEWHERE IN ENGLAND

Somewhere there must be music, and great swags of flowers,
leisured meals lasting for hours,
and smooth green lawns and roses.
Somewhere there must be dogs with velvet noses,
and people lounging in big chairs,
and bees buzzing in the pears.
So short a while, and yet how long,
how long,
since I was idling golden days away,
shopping a little and going to the play!
Somewhere the red leaves must be fluttering down,
but I am on my way to Kentish Town
in Mrs. Brodie's van,
which has no brakes and rattles like a can.
To-morrow I shall go to Wanstead Flats
with bales of straw, or a cargo of tin-hats,
or ninety mattresses to aid
the nether portions of the Fire Brigade.
Not for me a quiet stroll along the Mall,
I must be off to Woolwich Arsenal
with our Miss West;
and it seems I cannot rest,
there shall be no folding of my feet at all
till I have been to Islington Town Hall
with a buff envelope.
Some day it is my tenderest dearest hope
to have my hair washed, and I
would love to buy
something — anything so long as I could stop
for a moment and look into the window of a shop.
Somewhere there must be women reading books,
and talking of chicken-rissoles to their cooks;

but every time I try to read *The Grapes of Wrath*
I am sent forth
on some occupation
apparently immensely vital to the nation.
　　To my disappointed cook I only say
I shan't need any meals at all to-day.
　　Somewhere I know they're singing songs of praise
and going happily to matinées
and home to buttered toast,
but I at my post
shall bravely turn my thoughts from such enjoyment.
　　Ah for the time when, blest with unemployment,
I lived a life of sweet content —
leisured and smug and opulent!
　　Fear not, Miss Tatham, I am ready as you see,
to go to Romford Hospital or Lea.
　　Be not dismayed, I will not stray or roam,
Look how I fly to Brookwood Mental Home!
See with what patriotic speed I go
to Poplar, Ealing, Beckenham and Bow!

SOUND THE TRUMPET

If, said the Speaker, raising her voice in a rage,
(she was round about fifty years of age)
if you young girls in this country are going to shirk,
then all I can say is, by heaven, you must be made to work!
If you will not go voluntarily into the factories or join the Forces
then you must be driven there like horses!
　　We will not tolerate slackness, it is our duty to see
that every young woman under the age of thirty-three
is usefully employed making guns or aeroplane parts
and so on. There must be no excuses, no faint hearts.

The youth of England must show the world
why the Union Jack has never yet been furled!
If Russia can do it, surely we can do it too?
I want you — she pointed at the auditorium — and you and you!
   After a sip of water, the Speaker reluctantly resumed her seat,
and the women clapped vigorously and stamped their feet.
They were enthusiastic, they screamed each to each,
Wasn't that inspiring? Wasn't that a really *fine* speech?
     and they looked about them with ardent, burning eyes,
and the hall was filled with the sound of their battle cries,
and they beat their pointed umbrellas like tom-toms on the floor.
   (Their ages averaged, roughly, sixty-four.)

WHAT HAVE YOU DONE TO ME, ENGLAND?

So do I love the pleasures of the mind,
   Music and poetry, history and art,
It is not very nice for me to find
   That I'm a Blimp at heart.

For years and years I have not failed to laugh
   At Indian majors and their pukka wives
Who prop up British outposts during half
   Their chota-peggish lives.

England is always right, they think, and just;
   Foreigners are notoriously bad.
This obstinate, unthinking childish trust
   I have deplored, by gad!

Only a month ago, if you had said
   You had not heard of Brahms or Schopenhauer
I should have deemed you intellectually dead —
   Lower than any cauliflower.

O superficial windy gas balloon!
    When clouds of war were massed on the horizon
I blared more blimply than a brass bassoon
    Or any Indian bison.

Laying aside my thesis on the flute,
    I raised the good old Poona battle-cry:
'Line 'em against the nearest wall and shoot
    The lot of 'em!' said I.

Leaving my brethren of the highbrow fold
    To count the times they'd seen 'Aurora's Wedding',
Singing great hymns of praise I went and sold
    My soul to Lady Reading.

Listed in black and white to fight the foe,
    I stand a pariah in a world apart;
My friends avert their eyes for now they *know*
    That I'm a Blimp at heart.

TO THE GENTLEMAN IN ROW E

Dear Sir, we in Row E are well aware
Your soul is steeped in music to the core.
You love, we notice, each succeeding air
More deeply than the one which came before.

You lead the orchestra in perfect time,
With ever-nodding head you set the pace,
We in Row E consider it a crime
You are not in Sir Thomas Beecham's place.

Your lily hands most delicately haver,
Each phrase is ended with a graceful twist,
You know, it seems, each breve and semi-quaver,
And play them gently on your other wrist.

Sometimes you hum the least familiar portions,
And beat upon the floor a faint tattoo,
Though we can stand a lot of your contortions,
We shouldn't tap too much if we were you!

Dear Sir, we need no musical instructor,
We also sang in oratorio,
And if you were a really good conductor,
Our lightning would have struck you hours ago!

LADIES IN WAITING

Each in her separate house the young wives sit
   Alone from six to nine.
Though they be dear and beautiful and gay,
They never drink with friends or see a play,
   They never dance or dine.
Patient, the wives of Territorials sit and knit.

Straight from his work the model husband goes
   To distant dusty grounds.
Bathed in the ruddy setting of the sun,
He polishes a non-existent gun,
   Fires off imaginary rounds.
At home his wife droops like an autumn rose.

She droops, her proud head strangely, humbly bent
   Over a half-made sock.
Though she be fairer than a moonlit pool,
She points a cover for the piano-stool
   And sadly eyes the clock
So languorously ticking on impenitent.

When will he come, her love in dungaree,
   Back from his martial toil?
Starving, she sews away without a grumble
(The drawing-room echoes to her tummy's rumble)
   Haste, lover smudged with oil!
For here awaits a comfortless Penelope.

Oh, were the socks and jumpers lain out flat
   Together side by side,
With all the undies and the crocheted shawls,
They'd cover ninety times with ninety palls
   The heart of every bride
Who has to stay at home for once and tat!

23

EVENSONGS

When I am eighty-five and rather sweet,
  With knobbly hands and pince-nez, I shall sit
My children's children gathered round my feet,
  Dispensing wisdom, worldliness, and wit.

As I describe to them this far-off day
  Their tender laughs shall counteract my wheeze,
Their blue believing eyes will stare as they
  Lean on my unconfirmed and feeble knees.

'Tell us', they'll cry, 'about balloon barrages,
  And Mr. Chamberlain and Colonel Beck,
And cinemas and beacons and garages,
  And how Ruthenia got it in the neck.'

Well, I shall tell them something really fruity,
  Culled from the hazy dreams of might-have-been,
Of how I fought the Spaniards at Djibuti,
  And fled from Egypt with Queen Geraldine.

But when they ask me, as I fear they may,
  To sing them all the songs that once were sung,
How can my venerable trills convey
  The magic of the tunes when I was young?

How can I say to some enchanting boy
  His Grandpapa and I were wont to sing
'A Flat-foot Floogie with a Floy Floy'
  And 'Jeepers Creepers' and the 'Highland Swing'?

How can I bear to see his startled face,
  Who always thought his Granny sentimental
(A dove-grey figure swathed in yards of lace
  Quaveringly warbling something continental)?

Will he enjoy it when from out my bag
    I pull a mouth-organ, or perhaps a comb,
And give a rendering of the 'Tiger Rag'?
    'What about "Trees" ', he'll say, 'or "Home sweet Home" '?

Then I will lie, to make his childhood sweeter,
    And sing him bits out of the Cinema Star,
'Vilya', and 'A Little Pink Petti from Peter',
    'The Girl in the Taxi' and 'Under the Deodar'.

Yes, I will hum a bar or two of 'Sally',
    So badly that the boy is moved to tears;
And though I 'whiffenpoofed' with Rudy Vallee,
    I will gainsay it with the 'Gondoliers'.

1940

THE DEPRESSED BRIDE

I have come home now, down the sad dark street,
where heavy lie the greasy winter leaves.
Home! Our substantiated dream,
the freshly painted walls, the covers cream,
the yellow curtains hanging crisply new,
the pale unfurnished shelves with books askew.
A happy place, and yet my spirit grieves,
black as the mud about your Corporal's feet.

Here with the wedding silver I shall eat,
Calthrop will give me grouse your mother sent,
everything will be done to ease my lot,
the soufflé will be cold, the coffee hot.
Afterwards I shall climb the emerald stair,
sit with my knitting in a fire-lit chair.
Would I were buried in your soggy tent,
deep as the mud about your Corporal's feet.

SIR

Sir, will you kindly place under observance,
  A gentleman in your Department D.
Who, though no doubt the cream of Civil Servants,
  Has just been very, very rude to me!

Tell me of apes and peacocks,
of your life in Kalamazoo,
of how you opened the seacocks
when the raiders came in view.

Tell me of fire and murder,
and the time when you ran away
and lived with your aunt in purdah
somewhere in Mandalay.

Of the fishing rod and the bat and the gun,
of the mad wild days of your youth.
Speak to me as you've always done
with no regard for the truth.

Tell me your tales of desperate fights
with lions and jaguars;
of the seventeen days and eighteen nights
you spent behind prison bars.

Alas, you have got me cornered, caught,
so tell me exactly do,
what Gamelin said to General Gort,
and what both of them said to you.

I will listen, for I am kind of heart,
and your day is nigh its close;
but Edward dearest, before you start,
for God's sake blow your nose!

IF ONLY...

I know I could write music so entrancing,
   the nightingales would faint from off the trees,
I'd set the young girls singing, shouting, dancing,
   I'd make the old men hum like bumble-bees.

Oh lovely, lovely tunes! Some sweet, some gay,
   with violins soaring lark-high to the moon,
and some for brassy bands on holiday,
   and some to make the jitterbugsters swoon.

I'd bring a song of comfort to the lonely,
   I'd make the quietly-beating heart go boom,
I could be Brahms or Beethoven if only
   the piano wasn't in the other room.

DERRIÈRE PENSÉE

When I assumed the role of a vivandière,
and followed my husband to a seaside town,
I found myself recumbent on my derrière
in a boarding house bath. And it got me down.
   The water was not very hot, and the bath was peeling,
my towel, I knew, was only the size of a leaf;
and as I lay looking up at the smear on the ceiling,
I was filled with a dire and terrible grief.
   I will take my sponge, I said, and seek death.
   So I put it, not very comfortably, over my nose,
and immediately I was swooning under a scented breath.

Quite delicious! It was either the Essence de Rose
which I bought in Paris, or the Fleurs du Lac,
or else it was Roman Hyacinth. Or perhaps all of them subtly blended.
　　Whatever it was it took me surging back
to a life which is now forgot though so newly ended.
Yes, clinging through countless journeys to my sponge's cavities
were the dear memories of a strange far off world —
champagne, caviar, and other more modest depravities
such as facials, manicures, and hair weekly curled.
　　I saw myself sitting, elegantly dressed,
preening myself like a peacock for some sumptuous ball;
slowly I placed a splash of emeralds on my chest,
pinned to my hip a diamond waterfall,
went forth, rustling and cautious, careful of lips and hair,
my gloved hand lifting my cloak from off the floor,
and the sweet heady perfume followed me down the stair,
blown in great pungent wafts through the bathroom door.
　　When I assumed the role of a vivandière,
and followed my husband to a seaside town,
I found myself recumbent on my derrière
in a boarding house bath. And boy, did it get me down!

THE TAUNTON ROAD

I do not see how I can well forget
the little lambs new-born to Somerset,
who dance on rather wobbly woolly knees
in hilly fields beneath the quiet trees.
Spring is not far behind! A purple haze
hangs on the distant woods. O day of days!
O kindly Fate that bids me rise and ride
down catkin-studded lanes, through groves where hide
the simple snowdrops in the beds of moss!
O blessèd gifts of the American Red Cross!

The babies' bottles and the union suits,
the crateful of molasses and the boots.
The sky is white and blue, so I shall sing,
and come to Taunton with such news of Spring
I will appear like some immortal dove,
bringing them Wellingtons and soup and love!
O life divine, lived in a wagonette
among the little lambs in Somerset!

I GRIEVE FOR THE HAWAIIANS

I grieve for the Hawaiians,
　　Where blue seas run,
Lying like tawny lions
　　Stretched in the sun.

Though tenderly their fingers
　　Haunt the guitars,
Though honeyed perfume lingers
　　Under the stars.

Though flowers like crimson trumpets
　　Hang from the tree;
They have never, no never had crumpets
　　For Sunday tea.

FOUR LITTLE MILES

Four little miles, how long they lie
　　Between my love and me
Now that our startled eyes have seen
The gaping craters strewn between,
　　The rooms laid naked to the sky
Of homes that used to be!

Far, far away, and yet so near,
    My love beside his gun
Most fancifully thinks he sees
Incendiaries among my trees,
    While I, beneath the sofa hear
The bombs fall one by one

Upon his young defenceless head,
    As falls my coward's heart.
Oh, pity us who only share
The same bombardment from the air,
    Intolerable lumps of lead
Four little miles apart!

LET'S CHANGE THE SUBJECT

My thoughts are centred now on strange concerns.
No longer do I find my spirit yearns
To talk of theatres, or art, or books,
Or love affairs, or other people's cooks.
Dead as the dust of ancient dreams they lie,
And cannot comfort me, or edify.

But should you speak to me of bones, or tins,
Or swill for pigs, or sanitary bins,
My heart will leap to yours and in my eyes
The lust for aluminium will rise.
Ah me! A year ago I talked of Rome,
And Beatrice Lillie and the Hippodrome,

And roses and the Rhine and fruited trees
As yet unplundered by evacuees.

My conversation burgeoned forth and flowered
From Bach to Matthew Smith and Noel Coward;
I did not seek a restless bed afraid
I had forgotten to inform Miss Wade

That through some misdemeanour unforeseen
Some forty cups were gone from the canteen.
And now it seems, whatever may befall,
My life, my soul, my heart, my hands, my all
Are linked with sausage-rolls and wool and gauze,
Bound with old saucepans to the common cause.

FACE VALUE

Silent she sat in the vermilion chair,
  Her hands lay idle in her lap,
She stared at nothing in a deep dark sorrow
That loved not yesterday nor hoped for joy to-morrow,
  But wore the grief of ages like a wrap
    Lined with dismay, and pleated with despair.

Her mouth drooped sadly like a painted flower,
  White as a lily-bud her cheek;
Held rigid by some secret spell her magic
Eyes looked on a loveless world so starkly tragic,
  None, though he be compassionate, dared speak,
    Nor yet forgot the terror of that hour.

Oh heavy heart! Oh tired, unhappy head!
  What melancholy shades were these
That covered you with such a sombre awning?
What were you thinking of? 'Me?' she asked, loudly yawning;
  'I happened to be thinking about cheese,
    If that's of any interest,' she said.

32

MISSED OPPORTUNITY

Somehow I think we made a big mistake,
That time when we walked in the Spring twilight.
It was warm, I remember, and very clear,
And you stuck a primrose behind your ear,
And there was some sort of tree in blossom, white,
Reflected in the fly-dotted edge of the lake.

Somehow something tells me we missed the bus.
The moment is gone now, it is past recall;
But we walked there, in the sweetest scented breeze,
And I spoke, I know, at some length of evacuees,
And you of the maps you had pinned with flags to your wall.
I think, my friend, more than this was expected of us.

TO MY CAT, WELLINGTON

Wellington! These are solemn times in which we live,
a fact of which you seem to be acutely unaware.
No, I am not amused, not in the least, by these astounding attitudes,
so kindly rotate your head, that small white-whiskered ebon sieve
in my direction. Come and sit for a moment, quietly in a chair,
while I unload my soul of some maternal platitudes.

I know you are young, but nowadays that is quite a responsibility.
It isn't just having a good time. No, Wellington, *not* that!
You can have that afterwards. I want you to realize
that the life you lead is steeped in crass futility,
and that, at this rate, you'll never be the fine upstanding cat
your father and I have hoped and prayed for. Your amber eyes

should look more deeply into things; your foolish ears
listen to how the war is going and who it is between and who is
    winning.
I want you to stop boxing the daisies, stop bouncing in and out of
    doors;
I want you to be more sober, more serious as befits the years.
I want you—no, Wellington, listen—I want you, just as a beginning,
to sit quietly (*quietly* I said) on the rug, and wash your paws.

DO BRING YOUR VIOLIN

   Just for a start
let's play this lovely little Mozart.

You realize I haven't practised for ages?

Never mind. I will turn the pages.

Yes...

   Well, what about a Bach cantata,
or a Schubert sonata?
Both of them go rather slowly
because they are holy.

Oh dear. And we went oh
so lento!

   Well, would you care to try
Tosti's 'Good-bye'?
Or shall we have a go
at 'Poor Old Joe'?

That was grand,
but *why* only one hand?

Now this little thing was written
by Benjamin Britten,
supposedly for a flute and seven harps,
but it has no sharps
and the piano is silent after the first chord.
Oh Lord!

  No one can say
we do not play
'My Little Grey Home in the West'
with zest.

THE ANSWER'S IN THE NEGATIVE

Moistly, in the bathrooms of others,
a bit askew on the dripping walls
hang snapshots of sons and elder brothers
holding bats and balls.
  Above me as I wash, row upon row
stolidly sit the Poona Horse,
with names written neatly in ink below —
Sydney's is underlined of course.
  Dreary they are and most of them are dead;
a poor, poor form of mural decoration,
James and plain Priscilla getting wed,
Thomas as Member for the Isle of Dogs receiving an ovation.
  I also have a snapshot newly come
of Philip as a dewy Bombardier,
sitting with lots of other soldiers, dumb
horrible-looking men, tier upon tier.
  I will hang it on my bathroom's beautiful wall,
just like the others,
and not mind at all — alas! not at all.
So foolish are mothers.

No, dear, I will *not* eat in the scullery!
I will go down with my colours flying,
and the dining-room table shall be laid
with silver, bright and satisfying,
and glass and fruit and lemonade.

Though I be denied butter and butcher-meat,
and though there is no coal in the grate,
I will eat what I am allowed to eat
in pre-war dignity and state.

Not until I absolutely must
will I huddle in one room with all my relations,
relegating my furniture to decay and dust
and other such dilapidations.
My house shall be open wide as the air,
till it actually crumbles about my head;
and I shall sit in my sitting-room in a chair,
and sleep in my bedroom in a bed.
I cannot see why I should make life harder,
or indeed how it helps our Cause at all,
to spend the night on a camp-bed in the larder
and write letters in the servants' hall.

Till I am broke, which granted will be soon,
I will sometimes buy a gramophone record or a plant in a pot,
and I will not drink soup from a kitchen spoon,
no, really, dearest, I will not!

MY BONNY

(*To be sung to the old tune*)

My Bonny is stationed at ████
But nobody knows it, you see,
Except all the people of ████
And all his relations and me.

The ████ he is manning at ████
Sticks seventy feet in the air,
But don't tell a soul it's at ████
For *nobody* knows it is there.

LONDON NOCTURNE

To-night is a perfect night for lovers.
  There is a moon and stars,
No noise, no street lights,
  Jupiter, Venus, and Mars.

Thus it seems a pity for every wife,
  For every sweetheart and mother,
That all the men should be in one place
  And all the women in another.

AIR RAID

I laid me down on the hard cold floor,
  Heigho the holly!
From one A.M. to a quarter past four,
  O melancholy!
I heard the guns on the wild sea-shore
  Thunder and volley,
The beetles under the kitchen door
  Crept out for a jolly.
I laid me down on the hard cold floor
  Like a patient collie,
And wept for the unfathomable store
  Of human folly.

COMFORTLESS

(*With apologies to Austin Dobson*)

I intended a Sock
  And it turned to a Bonnet.
It was rather a shock,
It began as a Sock
But I just ran amok
  With the pattern, doggone it!
I intended a Sock
  But I *have* made a Bonnet.

NEW LOVE

I must learn now to love green things.
At last I must look on them with seeing eyes,
I, who have never loved the earth, nor the skies,
Nor heeded any nightingale that sings

In gardens more remote than Berkeley Square.
I have loved sunlight on the city street,
And the nocturnal thud of policemen's feet
Slapping the silence of the tar-stained air,

And noise, and lights, and little corner shops,
And fuggy cinemas and sooty rain;
Yet I will teach myself to love again —
Cattle and cornflowers and the crops.

Somehow I must attune my urban senses
To different sounds and different sights and smells,
To spiders' webs and Canterbury bells,
And tufts of sheeps' wool stuck on broken fences,

And stars! Yes, I will count the stars above,
And peer for tadpoles at the dark lake's side;
I will grow flowers, and only London Pride
Shall be the symbol of my former love.

THE EXILE

Had you informed me last July
that I
should like living in Bristol
(considering I was forced here at the point of a pistol),
I should have made some tart remark
and gone into the Park
vowing that I would be residing in a necropolis
before I left the Metropolis.

But Time, mean Time, has turned me fickle,
and with that sickle
of his
or scythe, or whatever it is,
he has cut, or at any rate undone
a lot of strings that bound my heart to London.

My house here is far, far uglier than sin,
gamboge without and chocolate fudge within.
The chairs are covered with an orange chintz
on which recline cushions of a violent quince
shade.

I am afraid
there are a million dinky nooks
in which hang large brass gongs on hooks.
The mantelpiece, beside which mellows
a quaintly painted pair of bellows,
is garnished with ladies standing on one toe in the buff
(made of some composite stuff)
and a china angel sitting on a boulder.
Upstairs we have Snow White as a toothbrush holder.

In the garden, behind alternate flowers, a gnome
has made himself an elfin home;
one cannot pick the tenderest of shoots
and fail to find a rabbit at its roots.

And yet and yet . . .
as I stand by the gooseberry net

of an evening and turn my face
to the barrage balloons and on, on to the place
where, in the blue shadows of the dying sun,
my love polishes his gun,
I know now that I could never leave Bristol
(except perhaps at the point of a pistol).

CAFÉ TRISTE

Miss Tomkinson, do you suppose
   That you and I
On this same day next year
Will still be sitting here,
   Eating this vegetable pie
Covered with white glucose?

Can you visualize with ease
   My ageing face
Suspended here before your eyes,
While moons set and suns rise,
   Bending towards the boiled plaice,
The potatoes and the peas?

Miss Tomkinson, do you suppose
   That next December
We shall pause at the soup-spoon's brink
And awfully dreadfully think
   Of the following November?
Oh, Miss Tomkinson, do you suppose?

IF

If you can go unswerving as an arrow,
Favouring neither foreigner nor friend,
If though the gate be straight, the pathway narrow,
You can pursue it to the very end,
If you can wait for those who lag behind you,
If you can gather strangers to your breast,
If the surbated traveller can find you
A home from home, an harbinger of rest.
If you are guided by some heavenly power,
Lit from within by a celestial light,
If you can keep your bearings hour by hour
However grey the day or dark the night,
If you can nurse the iron in your soul,
Finish the journey you have well begun,
Live on these lines till you have reached your goal,
You'll be a tram, my son.

AUTUMN LEAVES

The young soldier home on leave
 From his great gun
Sits by his wife's side
 In the autumn sun.

The tender words, the true,
 Will not be said,
They sit silent together
 And stare ahead.

That well-remembered song of love,
 So often sung,
Quivers but drowsily
 Upon the tongue.

The swift hours they share
   Are all too few,
Yet sleep drops on their eyes
   Like heavy dew.

Soon her lids close,
   Her head nods;
His mouth falls open a little
   Like a cod's.

The young soldier home on leave
   From his great gun
Sits by his wife's side
   In the autumn sun.

1941

AIR RAID OVER BRISTOL

The twelve Hurricanes circle round and round,
and we on the ground
stand in a little knot
and wait, even as they are waiting, for we know not what.
   A woman comes out of 'Chatsworth' and says:
'Anyone here seen Les?'
   'He's out in the van', says the grocer; 'went out
about
ten minutes ago', and then he rather surprisingly places
a pair of field-glasses to his eyes. We turn our faces
skywards again. Phew! What a sight!
   'Well, I hope he's all right',
says the woman, 'I hope he won't come to any harm.'
   I tuck my Salvage leaflets under my arm.

(Madam, do you keep your pig-food in a separate bin?
It is a sin
against the nation not to preserve each bone.)
Suddenly over the house-tops we hear a drone.
Dear Heavens, look at them! A hundred or more!
Wouldn't you say a hundred? I retire to the door
of a china shop. 'Hi, Mr. Bates, are they Jerries
or ours?' screams 'Sans Souci'. 'Jerries?'
taunts the grocer, peering through his glasses again.
'Good Lord, no, they're ours — positive.' With disdain
he smiles, 'I'd know ours anywhere'.
Immediately the air
is rent by wildest gun-fire. Across the sky
the twelve Hurricanes fly
like angry wasps. There is a lot of noise,
so, with what I hope is poise
I retreat into the china shop rather fast
and am at once cast
into a sort of iron dungeon under the stair-
case by the proprietress. Her mother is already there,
with a Tinies' night-light.
It is very hot and tight,
and I instantly realize we shall not survive,
and that I shall be buried alive.
Therefore I give a tremendously British smirk,
and say 'Oh, well, I suppose it's all in the day's work'.
Mother clicks her tongue and says 'It does seem a shame!'
and I remember I have not put my husband's name
on my identity card.
The floor is remarkably hard.
'Kit
will be having a fit
at school', says the proprietress, and gives a heave.
'They have *superb* shelters in *all* the schools, I believe',
I reply, and very carefully remove some candle-grease
from the crease

44

of my coat-lining.

    There is a shrill tormented whining
coming nearer and nearer,
clearer and clearer.
All that is British in me falters and flies,
I put my fingers in my ears and close my eyes.
It is aiming straight for the shop's portal.
We shall not die, we are immortal
(and, please, besides your dustbins
put, *separately*, all your tins).

    No, I am not dead, I feel well, and wonderfully clever.
The proprietress remarks appropriately, 'Well, I never!'
and crawls out on all-fours.

    We rush to the doors
to greet
'Chatsworth' and the others who are scouring the street
for shrapnel. They are oh, so merry.
Yes, it was a Jerry,
fell Fishponds way,
they say,

    'Well', I murmur, 'thank you so much, I mustn't stop.'
I bow to the proprietress of the china shop,
and now that I mysteriously feel such a credit to the nation
I hand her a leaflet on Salvage from the Corporation.

SLEEPING MIXTURE

When you're in bed to-night think not of wars,
 But rather of the Panda fast asleep,
Her piebald head cushioned on woolly paws;
 Or think of velvet mice that warmly creep

Into their holes to curl up round and soft.
 Transfer your thoughts from bellicose affairs;
Though it be true that bombers fly aloft,
 Try to reflect on little furry bears,

Slow drowsy summer sounds, the buzz of bees,
 A motor mower on some distant lawn,
Or pigeons cooing quietly in the trees.
 Ponder on dogs that sprawl about and yawn

In front of fires; or kettles hotly purring;
 Or gentle waves lapping a sandy bay.
Dwell not upon the form of Marshal Goering,
 Let not his image turn your night to day,

But think of things as round but more endearing —
 A puff-ball, or a large recumbent sheep,
Or stately, solemn, lazy clouds appearing
 To wrap you in an eiderdown of sleep.

LONDON TRAIN

I have imagined going to the station,
Heart purposely numb, mind studiously blunt,
To see my family cheerfully, bravely off
 To the battle-front.

In the night watches I have kissed them all good-bye,
I have waved to them, my husband and my brother,
But never did I dream the first to go
 Would be my mother.

HILFE! HILFE!

Hilfe! Hilfe! Komm, ich bitte, rasch!
Ich habe hier ein Nun mit ein Moustache!
Er sagt er ist ein Messenger of Friede
Dropt aus die Skies mit ein Velocipede,
Und hat ein freundlich Briefe mitgebracht
Addressed zu Mr. Churchill aus Herr Shacht.
Was kann ich sag? Man darf nicht sei *too* böse
Mit eine schwarz-begarbed Religieuse,
Es geht against das Korn zu sag er lugt
Und ist abscheulich, widerlich, verflucht!
Ich bete any Mensch wer hat ein Gun
Zu komm und hilfe me mit meine Nun!

ACHTUNG!

Was will ich tun wenn die Deutsche komm hier,
  Und klop an die Tür von mein Haus?
Will ich yellen Sie können nicht stehen bei mir,
  Or will ich bleib dumb wie ein Maus?

Velleicht für ein Frau es ist besser zu try
  Eine farbelhaft Siren zu sein,
Zu offen die Tür mit ein willkommen Shrei,
  Und cracken ein Flasche von Wein.

Mit weibliche cunning ich könnte, ich dink,
  Ein dope zubemix mit das Port,
Und erstlich enbeten die Herren zu trink,
  Dann kling für das Heimguard sofort!

Aber nein! Als ein Bosch legt ein Fuss in mein Land,
  Ich soll sei so böse, ich glaubt
Ich will hastliche nehmen das Poker im Hand,
  Und bangen der Schwein on die Haupt!

FADE OUT

I doubt if we shall meet again, Miss Sergison-Moffat,
    When the guns have ceased firing, and the bomb-racks are empty
      once more,
For I shall return, swift as the feathered arrow to London,
    And you will go back to your garden and the round hills you adore.

The broad grey river that runs through your life will still be there,
    And there the broad grey pavements will be waiting, please God,
      for me;
And neither of us will dare to part from them for an instant,
    None will be quite so madly wildly jealous of their loves as we.

You will forget me utterly, Miss Sergison-Moffat,
    And yet, I think, you will pause every now and then and turn your
      head;
The sight of a soup-urn or the bitter smell of moth-balls
    Will conjure to your mind scenes you thought buried deeper than
      the dead.

'H'm', you will say, snapping your fingers, 'now what *was* her name? . . .
    Ethel, you remember, that woman who drove the big American van?
She used to carry enormous parcels, *far* too heavy,
    And had a husband in the Anti-Aircraft, such a nice young man —'

And then, brushing the thought aside, you will turn back again
    To feast your gentle eyes on whatever happens to be in flower,
For these heavy chains that yoke us together in war-time,
    Will be light as thistledown on our shoulders in the peaceful hour.

SWITCH IT OFF!

Any news on the wireless to-day? . . .

   Nothing to speak of, Madam.
Only a few bombs here and there
(they didn't, of course, say exactly where) —
Oh, we've lost some planes in a raid off Crete,
and ten small ships of the Merchant Fleet.
They say there's a billion men in Russia
fighting a billion men from Prussia,
and hundreds are dying like flies in the sand
in Libya and the Holy Land . . .

Thank you, May, so there isn't much news?

   Nothing to speak of, Madam.

VALE!

Before they fade for ever from our sight,
Sailing like ghostly ships into the night,
Let there be one luxurious hour in which
We pause awhile to contemplate the rich.

Consider them once more before they pass
Into a more unfashionable class,
Though it is true their loss shall be our gain,
Weep, for we shall not see their like again.

Let us be honest now, and testify
That many of them pleased the outward eye,
Their cars and yachts were lovely to behold,
Beauty they bought, and colour, with their gold.

And oh! Their houses, rising from the green
Of peacocked lawns more smooth than velveteen.
Palladian porticos, and warm pink towers
Set in a scented sea of English flowers.

D

Slandered so joyfully throughout the years,
Unmourned they go, unwashed by any tears
From eyes that once were strained to witness capers
Cut for their benefit in weekly papers.

Thus they depart into a strange new land,
Speaking a tongue, they do not understand;
So for a little moment, with regret,
Let us remember them — and then forget.

OVERTURE FOR BEGINNERS

Oh, mourn for those who had songs to sing
   And have sung their songs to sleep;
For the muted reed and silent string,
   For the muffled keyboard, weep;

For the poet, whose shadowy half-dreamed rhymes
   Before they were born had died;
Oh, grieve for the crimson lakes and the limes,
   And the brushes laid aside.

Theirs now the music of great machines,
   The ballad of steel upon steel;
Theirs the poetry of submarines,
   The art of the turning wheel.

Beauty they seek in the cannon's roar,
   Truth in the barrack square,
Grace in the steel-grey birds that soar,
   Joy in the falling flare.

Pause to remember them now and then,
   The workers at home and abroad,
Who fight in the faith that the brush and the pen
   Are mightier than the sword.

1942

EVENING

As the dark day moves into darker evening,
    and the pale pin-pointed lamps are lit in the street,
as the typists stand shivering by the bus-stop,
    wreathed in their warm breaths, stamping their cold feet

on the greasy pavements — I seem to see manifested,
    hanging like a foggy aura above their tired heads,
the word Home. I feel the surge of their silent yearning,
    all hearts turned towards fires and food and smooth beds.

This is the sweet hour of expectation.
    Only a little while and they will have forgotten this;
only a little while and the day will be drowned
    in the sound of a child's voice, the touch of a lover's kiss.

Their senses will be washed by music for the Forces,
    the cheerful clanking of plates, the running of taps;
and they will sit talking, or nodding over a cup of tea,
    with books and knitting and drowsy cats in their laps.

These are their wages, the true fruits of their labour,
    valued above all things, above dreams or ambitions or careers,
for a job can be lost, and another as easily forgotten,
    but Home is carried tenderly, like a babe, throughout the years.

The darker evening moves into darkest night.
    The typists change their attaché cases to the other hand;
they turn up their coat-collars and sigh;
    they put their papers under their arms, and stand,

As the buses thunder by with lidded eyes,
    the queues wait sombrely in their appointed places,
but I see the great lights that are lit for a homecoming
    blazing like beacons on their patient faces,

ODE ON A THERMOT URN
(with apologies to Keats)

Thou still impure slave of thirstiness,
 Thou foster child of mutton broth and tea,
How can a dictionary of words express
 The inspissated gloom you raise in me!
What pungent legends hang about thy form,
 Of bitter rooms where Chaos reigned supreme,
Where women wept amid the Salmon Spread,
 Where weary kettles vainly sought to steam
On gasless rings; and soups that would not warm
 Stood in congealéd pools among the bread.

What visions dost thou conjure to my mind!
 What scenes of sordidness do haunt thee yet,
Of streets laid waste, of hoses intertwined
 Of tired grave people trudging through the wet.
I cannot look at thee and fail to smell
 The sickening odour of a burning town:
I hate thee so! And yet do I discern
 Draped on thy lid a little starry crown,
Laid there by firemen who have loved thee well,
 And blessed thee, O most deep and dirty urn.

'DESPISE NOT PROPHESYING...'

If, in 1933,
you had said to me
Virginia, old sock, I see it all planned,
it is written in your horoscope and in your hand
that in 1942
you
will find yourself sitting one night,
feeling quite

outstandingly pipped
in the crypt
of a Bristol church . . . you will be leaning in a dump
over an object called a stirrup pump,
wearing your husband's trousers and a travelling rug,
and drinking tepid coffee out of an enamel mug —
    Stop! I should have said,
listen, my sweet, you are ill, you must go to bed
at once! Now don't get in a rage,
but it looks as if you're getting to the pink elephant stage,
so be a good chap and throttle
down on the bottle.
    Or I might have said Chucks!
or Sucks!
but I should never, never,
however
much it grieved you,
have said I believed you.

Which only goes to show,
said she, again (alas) rolling off the li-lo.

RUMOUR

    Let us not think about it!
Oh, vain, vain to curb the thoughts that stray,
Leaping ahead to greet the unnamed day . . .
Tell me again what did the General say,
    That I may doubt it.

    You might be posted where?
No, no, such happiness can not be mine,
The very word is headier than wine.
Away, winged vision of the Serpentine,
    Most blessèd Leicester Square!

I must not plot nor plan.
Nor in my mind unsheet the drawing-room chairs,
Nor Hoover madly up and down the stairs . . .
Speak to me of the world and its affairs,
   Distract me if you can.

   Let us rise far above it!
Talk of the sights we've seen, the books we've read . . .
But, if you please, before we go to bed
Tell me just once more what the General said
   That I may love it.

RETREAT

When there is peace again, soldier, what will you do?
   I shall go back to the job I had before
   Behind the counter at the hardware store —
      That's what I'll do.

And you, sailor, when you have left the sea?
   I shall go back to my job as a plumber's mate,
   And lean of an evening on my garden gate —
      That'll suit me.

What will you do, brave man with the silver wings?
   I shall return, I hope, to my pre-war life,
   To my dog and my week-end golf and my wife
      And such like things.

And I myself, what is my heart's desire?
   I want to go back to a house that is all mine,
   To lie in one of my own chairs on my spine
      By the fire.

Back, back, is where all of us want to go,
   Each to his little well-worn well-loved spot;
   So who in the wide world's going forward is what
      I'd like to know?

LOOK!

Look! Whoopee!
This is me
on a motor-bike!
Isn't it smart? I feel like
goodness only knows what.
I bet you'd give a lot
to be me?
   Whee!
  This is the first time I have ridden
such a thing, and nearly all the knobs and levers are hidden
mysteries to me; so you see I am rash,
I am wild, I am wonderful, I am cutting a dash.
   Oh the glorious air!
Oh the wind in my hair!
Delightful! Doesn't it look delightful?
(As a matter of fact it is rather frightful,
as cold as ice.)
  I have already stopped the engine twice,
but a postman and a boy got it started
again and I am very brave. I am lion-hearted.
I go *swish* and *swoosh* and *zoom* and *splutter*.
I just happen to be in the gutter
at the moment because I cannot make up my mind
whether I will stay behind
this bus or come out with a great roar.
Really there are more
buses in this town, and mad dogs, and imbecile
old ladies teetering about in front of my wheel!
   But I do not care,
I am all that is gay and debonair;
I am the eagle that soars and the arrow that flies;
I am a golden-haired goddess with eyes
like sapphires; I am a crusader
sent by heaven to outwit the invader.

I can see myself crouched over the handlebars,
hurtling through the night under the stars,
bearing a letter like a St. Bernard in my strong white teeth —
good news from Bristol to Crewe, bad news from Bath to Leith.
   I will be Jehu personified;
like a dragon I will eat up the countryside.
Oh the singing and the shouting and the cheering and the crying
as I ride through with my coat-tails flying!
   Look at me now! I am going fast!
The trees go *wham wham* as I race past,
I am burning them up like a forest fire!
   No, but surely, this speedometer has gone completely haywire,
it registers only nineteen miles an hour!
   Hand me a lemon, some one, pluck me a flower!

OUR WINTER COLLECTION

Cet hiver, madame, on va porter, je crois,
   Des confections assez singulières,
Mais même si elles ne seront pas très chic, ma foi,
   Elles seront, je vous le promets, très chères!

Laissez-moi vous montrer, de la part de notre maison,
   Quelques petites choses qui vous plairont, j'en suis sûre —
Voici, madame, une ravissante combinaison,
   Tricotée d'une laine étrangement dure.

Cette chemise de nuit, fabriquée d'une souple flanelle,
   Elle a du chien, n'est ce pas, avec ses manches bouffantes?
On les offre en deux couleurs, gris ou miel,
   Et ça vous garantira une nuit vraiment étouffante.

Regardez, madame, cette jupe d'une simplicité exquise,
  D'une serge bleu marin — très jeune, très écolière!
Et je parie que Madame aura l'air d'une Marquise
  Dans ce balaclava de poil de dromadaire.

A la fin, je vous offre, comme pièce de résistance,
  Des sabots! Une plaisanterie extrêmement gaie!
Ils sont d'une incommodité immense,
  Mais là-dedans vous marcherez vers la paix.

SLEEP

The most beautiful thing in the world to-day is sleep.
We had other loves once, but now this is the dearest, the best,
The dark-blue velvet wave that bears us deep
into strange unbelievable places where man is still blessed;
to flowered fields where we stand bent with laughter;
to white beaches where we lie without a care;
wherever we go the people we have loved follow after,
our mothers and fathers, our friends, and even our dogs are there.

Sleep despises the years. It cares not for time or space.
In its arms we know for certain there is life without death.
There are no barriers. We go without moving from place to place;
the past, the present, and the future can be lived in a breath,
and countries conquered before the end of a sigh,
and meetings and partings and songs and loves be ours as we turn
in our narrow beds where our shadowy bodies lie.

Sleep is a beautiful thing, and kind. It does not spurn
the stupid, the ugly, or the faint at heart.
The foolish shall seek it and find it again and again,
and though it cannot be won by wisdom or wit or any proven art,
even the wicked man shall not woo it entirely in vain.

SUNSET

There's nothing so sad in the world as to stand alone
On a velvet lawn at the end of a summer's day,
Watching the purple shadows fall,
Hearing the distant ping of a tennis-ball,
The sound of happy voices calling 'Away!'
A thrush singing. A rose full blown.

Indoors they are clinking the spoons, the baths are run;
Nanny looks cheerfully out of the window at the sky,
It will be fine, she says, to-morrow.
Oh, but the strange unfathomable sorrow
Of croquet mallets leaning on hoops awry,
And crumpled cushions crimsoned by the sun.

They will come home by way of the gooseberry-nets.
No spell can bind them who are young and brave
To this most melancholy hour,
When hope dies, and fear bursts into flower,
When the heart illogically seeks its grave,
Stabbed by incomprehensible regrets.

IT'S ALL VERY WELL NOW

It's all very well now, but when I'm an old lady
I think I shall be amazed, and even a bit annoyed maybe,
when I look back at these years of ceaseless effort
and consider what I did to keep my country free.

If only I were making munitions, or had joined the Forces,
my grandchildren, I know, would not think I'd fought in vain,
by why on earth I did some of the things I am doing now
will be so terribly tiresome to explain.

How can I convince them that it was to England's good
that I went to Waterloo to meet two goats travelling from Camberley,
and drove them in a car across to Victoria, where I put them in another
  train,
third class, non-smoker of course, to Amberley?

Why, do you suppose, when London was burning,
did I find myself alone with a Church Army lady from Rye,
and why did we do nothing at all except drink port and lemon?
(She had a dish-cover on her head, tied on with a Zingari tie.)

And will my children believe me when I tell them
that I carried a flame within me that no mortal power could dowse,
not even when I was made to take a vanload of corsets and molasses
to confuse already hopelessly confused Admirals at Trinity House?

I must confess I sometimes get a bit confused myself.
Why am I doing this? I ask and wonder — why in Britain's name did
  I do that?
Did I really imagine it would lead us grimly forward to Victory
to share my smoked-salmon sandwiches with the Home Office cat?

All my little war stories will sound so frivolous.
'The old lady is getting very frail,' they will say — 'very soft in the
  brain';
But I shall nod my head and say, 'Believe me, my children,
in my young days everybody was automatically quite insane'.

THE SECOND FRONT

I am fighting on my own a lonely battle.
  Gallant, and oh, so lonely do I stand,
Facing the thunderous batteries of Spring,
  The tarnished sword of Conscience in my hand.

They are slowly creeping up on every side,
  The blossom and the birds and the young grass;
But through the bent bastion of my resolve
  I swear on England's name they shall not pass.

Let them bombard me with their nightingales,
  Though I may listen, yet I will not hear;
Let them lay mines of primroses and moss,
  My feet shall tread between them without fear.

I know so well their treacherous infiltrations.
  Spring in the blood! That galvanizing urge
To buy up every single mortal thing,
  From foolish hats to dreary lengths of serge.

Insidious and warm, the balmy air
  Bids me be lavish with my dwindling gold
As are the buttercups, 'gainst whose suggestive flames
  The pumps of thrift I have avowed to hold.

The trees like frothy quislings stand bedecked,
  Whispering 'Spend, and you will look like us!'
I face the blowing of their scented guns
  With Duty as my rusty arquebus.

I shall prevail if I am brave and true;
  But oh, how glorious the opposition!
And oh, to fight so heavenly a foe
  With such intensely boring ammunition!

PANIC

This is the darkest hour of my drab little life!
You remember that letter full of important enclosures for Miss Maxse?
Well, it's disappeared! Plainly speaking, I have lost it,
and I intend to go straight out and lie down in front of a taxi.
    You are not being at all amiable, not at all sympathetic.
Is it nothing to you that my hair has turned two shades whiter?
If you are unable to make the correct compassionate noises,
at least you might have the grace to look under your typewriter!
    Now I put it *here* — no I didn't, it was *there*;
I pinned it to the table with the edge of my Out tray,
unless, of course, I put it *in* to the Out tray, which would considerably
    clarify matters.
    (I simply do not see how I can survive to-day.)
    Would you be courteous enough to raise your feet?
I wish to look under that obscene little mat of yours.
It would appear that your friendship for me does not go the length
of seeking for lost things on all fours.
    Do not smile. You would not smile if you had lost Miss Maxse's
    letter!
(By the way, just see if it is stuck to that pot of glue?)
    If only I thought she would strike me savagely across the face with
    some blunt instrument!
But she will be kind, I know, and my heart will break in two.
    Very well then, it is lost, and I will pay the supreme penalty.
Every folly, we are told, is bought at a price;
and doubtless when they are dragging the static water troughs for my
    body,
you will be sorry — it will not be at all nice.
    I am going now, my friend, here is my wrist-watch and my badge,
here is a piece of snow-white hair to wear round your neck in a locket,
and here, as a matter of fact, is Miss Maxse's letter,
which some great fool must have put in my overcoat pocket!

BERSERK

Madam, it's no use looking at me like that!
Yes, I have bought a red carnation.
So what, madam, so what?
Incidentally, old pie-face, this is a new hat,
the very latest innovation,
believe it or not.
    And in case you're interested and want to know
what I am carrying in my hand,
old nosey that you are!
they're gramophone records, all of them low
tunes played by a hot sweet band
beating them, daddy, eight to a bar.
    Maybe you've got a perfect right to stare.
There's a war on, and who's got the money
to spend on some fading finite thing?
But by heavens, madam! can't you smell the air,
the new-mown grass and the flowers and the honey?
Have you never heard of Spring?
Poor old sour-puss, have you forgotten Spring?

BATH

To-morrow I shall go to Bath. I shall leave my duties,
however nationally important, far behind me
and I shall go to that proud quiet city.
There will I be. There you will find me.

I shall climb up Gay Street where Fanny Burney stayed,
and pause in the Circus at the top of the hill,
Disregarding the admirals and the ladies in small fur hats,
my tired eyes shall drink their fill.

I will go to Royal Crescent and think of the Prince Regent.
The Prince Regent and I will look at that perfect semi-ellipse;
though there be a warden's post there, or static water,
such shining beauty can suffer no eclipse.

The lovely balconies and the big wide windows,
the broad curving sweep of the roadway from end to end
will remind me that whatever I say, and I say a great deal,
this is what I am fighting to defend.

Let me stand quietly there and think of quiet things;
or if I cannot think, then let me stare.
For if the hand truly fashions what the heart desires,
here man is not forsaken, here I need not despair.

Down Milsom Street, shadowed by Beau Nash,
shadowed by Jane Austen and Doctor Oliver and William Pitt,
I will wend my way, peacefully and gratefully remembering
elegance and biscuits and kindly wit.

To-morrow I shall go to Bath. Yes, there you will find me,
having a nice hot cup of tea in Quiet Street.
And my soul will be as quiet too as a limpid pool,
as quiet as a grey dove my soothed heart's beat.

DESPONDENCY AND ALARM

   I have counted my blessings one by one,
starting in the orthodox fashion with the sun,
And God's good air and the trees,
and flowers, of course, and, I suppose, bees.
   I have complimented myself upon having a husband and a cat
both of astonishing charm — and for that matter a mat
for the cat to sit on. I have friends.
Health and youth pay me stout dividends;

my house, though deserted, is intact,
in fact
everything in the garden's dandy.
  I even have some American candy,
and three-quarters of a pot of marmalade,
and we haven't had a raid
for a long time.
  I'm
counting my blessings one by one,
counting out loud the things I've done,
this and that and the other.
  Thank God for Mother.
  Thank God I'm not dead.
  Thank God people have said
warm and wise
things. Thank God for ears and eyes.
  Oh, but I wonder why
I'd like to sit down and have a nice good cry!

1943

HOPE

No faith in the hour of betrayal,
  No scorning of lions' jaws,
No heart of grace in the battle-field,
  No faith in a faithless cause,
No hope in the days of bondage
  Has ever more valiant shone
Than the hope that hopes for a taxi
  When the last bus has gone.

OFFICE STOOGES

If in the humble darkness of our minds ideas are lurking,
   It is neither meet nor proper to bring them to light;
For we are the people who come in on Saturday morning,
   We are the people who wait for the telephone to click off at night.

Let us not try to be clever. The country could not stand it.
   There are enough wizards already having lunch till three;
And we are the people who check ledgers and run errands,
   We are the people who buy paper-clips and brew those nice cups of
      tea.

If we feel we would dabble in matters of high policy
   Let us remember there are dozens clustering on the ropes.
Not for us the strategy planned on the 4.10 to Hitchin;
   We are the people who do the black-out and stick stamps on
      envelopes.

Though there is nothing hid from us, though we have all knowledge,
   The war cannot be won if we insist on being bright;
For who could they find to come in on a Saturday morning?
   Who could they find to wait for that damned telephone to click off
      at night?

WE WHO ARE QUITE OLD

We have become as little children again,
we who are quite old.
Monday is the most horrible day of all,
and Sunday is gold.
   On Saturday mornings our offices are dreamy,
and thoughts take wing
to concerts and cinemas and walks in the park;
we tend to sing.

But when the last crumpet is eaten at Sunday tea,
our spirits fall
as they fell when we had forgotten to do our homework
when we were small.
We have become as little children again.
We start and blush
when spoken to by our superiors;
we even flush
in the dark watches of the night when we remember
duties undone;
oh, and on Sunday our young-old hearts go down, down, down
with the setting sun!

THE BRIDGE, ST. JAMES'S PARK

You cannot find comfort in ducks.
Stoop to look into those beady brown eyes,
and they will tell you nothing.
Lean over the bridge and the reflected leaf-brown skies
quiver and fade as the little copper head
swims to your shadow;
and as he looks jauntily at the pond's bed
over that soft grey breast of his, you think
this duck knows something.
I am standing at the brink
of some sweet secret which will bountifully bless.
From the quirk of his tail I shall learn gaiety,
and though I cannot caress
the velvet roundness of his feathered hair,
I shall see in it the perfection of small things,
beauty of burnished copper warming the air,
satin-smooth order in the midst of confusion.
But in those flat eyes there lies no understanding or hope,
only a deadly cynicism, an utter delusion.
You cannot find comfort in ducks.

I REMEMBER, NOT SO LONG AGO

I remember, not so long ago
    There was magic in the air,
I felt it in strange unexpected places,
    And now it is not there.

I can stand on the Serpentine Bridge
    While the sun sinks low,
But the trees are trees, and Harrods is Harrods:
    This was not formerly so.

Musicians tuning their instruments
    Before a concert begins
Are ordinary gentlemen in dark suits
    Playing on violins.

I can hear old songs sung.
    I am not stirred
By a faded letter or a falling star
    Or the call of a bird.

Tugboats ahoot on the river
    At the break of day
Are hooting because there are other tugboats
    Riding in the way.

I remember, not so long ago,
    There was magic in the air,
And though it has gone with the lights and laughter
    I know it is still there.

LEBENSRAUM

I had a bedroom where I slept for twenty years.
It was all mine from roof to floor,
from floor to door.
It knew me as I was, my loves and fears,
and bore the scars and fancies of my age.
    The fire-guard where Nanny warmed my socks,
cress growing in a cardboard box,
two lovebirds in a cage,
my height marked in pencil on the wall,
large pink sea-shells gathered here and there,
a china pot from Weston-super-Mare,
a dented ping-pong ball.
    These were all swept away and in their stead
blossomed on mantelpiece and table
photographs of Clark Gable.
Jack Buchanan swung above my head,
and I would lie there in the foolishness of youth,
gloriously sad and infinitely wise,
seeking the limpid eyes
of Greta Garbo to discover Truth.
    The years passed, and I would come at night,
home from the ballroom and its floodlit gold
to the quiet cold
of shadowed objects in the hanging light;
and I would dream and sigh and dream again
in this small space that was my very own.
Alone, alone,
I wept my tears on to the counterpane,
as now my exiled heart in patience weeps;
for in that room so much a part of me,
a Major in the H.A.C.
combs his moustache and cleans his teeth, and sleeps.

LOVE IS A TENDER PLANT

Love is a tender plant, yet it grows in the strangest places.
Slums, factories, docks cannot gainsay it,
No layers of the blackest dirt can conceal its budding
        Or slay it.

Tho' we know its delicate flower may bloom in a tenement,
And to the lowliest breast be pinned on,
Surely it must be terribly hard to fall in love
        In Swindon.

HARVEST FESTIVAL

My brain is a bog, and in it there are planted
   Seeds bought with money at a fair price,
Education, experience, and a packet of travel,
   Taste and intelligence and good advice.

They were planted faithfully, a long time ago,
   On a trim, well-weeded, well-watered bed,
And it was hoped by now there would be a fine harvest,
   But other things have blossomed in their stead.

There are no tall hollyhocks to mark the border,
   The red roses have died — they were a total loss,
Only the bog-myrtle is blowing and the wild thyme,
   And everywhere the heavy dripping moss.

There is no promise now of carnations or lilies,
   But here is a little bunch that will live for an hour:
Marsh-marigolds and mint and water-plantains,
   And sprigs of duckweed bursting into flower.

A PRAYER

O Ceres, from whose copious horn
flows the gold corn,
the young lettuce and green
pea, the mushroom, the bean,
the sweet red cherry,
the new potato and the strawberry —
Thou, from whom life itself so bounteously comes,
please, *please*, PLEASE no more plums!

SEA WRACK

I am going to the grey sea,
To the gulls beating their curved wings
against the clouds;
to the short tufted grasses,
lying like pads on the dunes;
to the wind flying its salty banner
sprayed with sapphires,
over the wild skies,
over the stars.
    Away, away I will go
to the loneliness of the little pools
where the redshanks meditate
with bright eyes;
and none shall come nigh me,
none shall know where I am or care.
    Dear Lord in heaven,
how I shall hate it there!

TO MARIA

When the war is over and done with,
    And what is still to be has been,
I shall look forward to seeing you, my friend,
    With a face less green.

Five years ago it was circular
    And, like a baby mushroom, pink.
There were no beetles then on your brow,
    And almost no ink.

Among the many things Hitler has done
    Which have signally failed to please
Is the metamorphosis of your face, Maria,
    Into a green cheese.

MAUD'S CHILDREN

Maud, in her long feathered trousers,
broods lovingly over her bantam chicks,
counting them aloud (rather tiresomely) all day,
one, two, three, four, five *and*, believe it or not, six!

Their small brown velveteen bodies
bounce about in aimless animation;
they hop up and down, and scream things to each other
in high-pitched voices trembling with indignation.

To judge from their state of turmoil,
all are presumably catching last trains,
as breathlessly, still shouting instructions, they race
tripping over things, into the darkness of drains,

only to reappear half crazed
by the ghastly things they have nearly seen,
to gallop, with smothering sobs into the soon-
discovered ghastliness of the threshing machine.

With great difficulty they climb
on to Maud's back, stagger groggily round,
peer vertiginously over her wings and then
closing their eyes, fall with a shrill shriek to the ground.

They spin and slip up and slither
like a crowd of hysterical skaters,
and though I know they are dear Maud's children they look
like mentally deficient bumblebees in gaiters.

A PLEA FOR MERCY

Oh, take those dear old ladies off their bicycles!
   I cannot bear to see them any more,
Pedalling slowly, slowly down the Mall,
   Beating their way up Knightsbridge and the Gore.

Let those old legs that turn like tired tops
   Be stretched out straight in sumptuous motor-cars;
And white heads raised to rest on downy pillows,
   Which now are bent over the handlebars.

Let them be wrapped in rugs and driven forth
   As precious as bright jewels in a casket,
To bring the haddock home in ease and splendour,
   Instead of in a little wicker basket.

Oh, dreadful years, that bid our grannies ride
   Like aged Amazons unconquered still
On rusty steeds to fight a losing battle
   Against the grade of Constitution Hill!

IN COLD STORAGE

As beautiful as mountains in the morning,
 Stately and splendid still, and still unsold,
The houses of the rich are very handsome,
 And also very, *very*, VERY cold!

The fresh keen wind that whistles through the doorways,
 Freezes the Toulouse-Lautrecs to the walls,
And lumps of snow drift with the bills from Asprey
 Across the ice-green hyperborean halls.

The brandy glasses and the Rockingham
 Rattle with palsy on the Empire tables,
And little moths, newborn, are frozen solid
 To die, amazed, upon the minks and sables.

With diamond rings concealed in lambskin gloves,
 With pearls and mufflers strangely intertwined,
In small back rooms, looking on sad grey leads,
 The opulent sit cowering and resigned.

The Adam mantelpiece bends slightly over
 To warm its emblems in the timid fire,
And oh, how bitter true it is, the saying,
 None but the impecunious perspire!

On to the landings, where their breath in clouds
 Floats round the fluted banisters, the dead
Rich, who have lost what money cannot buy,
 Put on their skis and clamber up to bed.

AUNTS

Children, when you have gone your several ways,
and have sought the long days'
happiness, and the night's elusive dream,
incredible as it may seem
you will turn, at some moment, like thirsting plants
to your aunts.
  Now, aunts are not glamorous creatures,
as very often their features
tend to be elderly caricatures of your own.
Aunts use eau-de-cologne
and live in rather out-of-the-way places,
and wear pointed white shoes with laces
tied in a neat bow.
  Oh, I know, I know!
  Nevertheless I maintain
that when you are old enough to learn pain,
are acquainted with sorrow, and know what fear is,
your aunts will not seem nearly such drearies.
  You'll see,
believe me!
  When you've broken off your engagement and want to hide,
you will go to Aunt Beatrice at Ambleside.
When the charwoman falls down dead,
Aunt Edith will give you a bed.
When your heart breaks, as hearts sometimes do,
Aunt Constance at Looe
will feed it on Cornish cream and philosophy,
soothe it with strawberries for tea;
and when, with the dew still behind your ears
you set forth to conquer wider spheres,
I do not think you will get much further the first night
than Aunt Maud in Shanklin, Isle of Wight.
  Oh, yes, children, aunts are kind
and quite resigned

to the fact that you will not go near them for years,
and then bring them your tears.
Although at your tender age
you resent their neglect of the Stage,
their inability to differentiate between jazz and swing,
and their poor reactions to Bing,
the day will dawn when they will rise up like rocks,
sheltering you with their long imprimé frocks
and cornflowered hats worn at such hopeless slants —
your nigh-forgotten, soon-remembered aunts.

NANNY

Where is my Nanny in her long grey coat and skirt,
   and a black straw hat stuck with a pin to her head?
Where has she gone with her creaking petersham belt,
   and the strange, flat, comforting, senseless things she said?

'Cheer up, chicken, you'll soon be hatched!' she would tell me,
   drying my ears in a rough methodical way,
and 'Mark my words, it'll all come out in the wash',
   and 'It's just Sir Garnet Wolseley!' she used to say.

I still don't know what she meant, but oh, it was nice
   to hear that distrait voice so ruggedly tender,
as glimmering starchily she would cross the room
   to hang my liberty bodice on the fender.

Would she were here on this perilous bomb-scarred night,
   as warm and satisfying as a loaf of bread,
to stand like a round shield between me and the world,
   to give me a bath and carry me up to bed.

SATURDAY MORNING OFF

This is the sort of morning I could eat!
Take Oxford Street
for instance. It is golden and crisp,
with just a wisp,
a feathery faint-brown smell in the pallid air
of burning leaves in Cavendish Square,
like home-made caramels. Oh, heaven,
these hours stolen from Mr. Bevin!
(Such sad sweet hours,
fleeting as flowers,
held in the mind for many a desk-bound day,
so soon away.)
Let there be singing, for the sun shines,
and the shop signs
clank in the wintry wind with hopeful news;
even the patient queues
waiting for hake and beer and liquorice gums
glow in the tawny light of chrysanthemums;
and the buses are red . . . yes, yes, but to-day
they are *redder*. And gay, gay, gay
is the world, a little round bundle of bliss!
Never before was there quite such a morning as this

GRATITUDE

Did you *hear* the bombers, for heaven's sake?
Ye gods above, I should just hope it *was* a mistake!
Why in the name of all that's holy did they have to take
this route? As if life wasn't hellish enough already
do they have to go and make
that b— row all night. Made the whole ruddy place shake!
Dammit all, I know that, but they kept me *awake*!

THE PARTY

The chrysanthemums lay in yellow pools on the tables,
Their bitter smell rose up with the curling smoke
of lazy cigarettes, and the fire's bright burning
shone on the glasses quietly raised and lowered.
    The friendly heads rested on the backs of sofas,
and hands, white in the lamplight, stretched forward for matches.
    Somebody played the piano and somebody sang,
cool as the far stars on an autumn night,
clear as a rocky pool left by the tide,
sweet as a young bird on a holiday.
    And oh, my heart, my heart remembered its old beating,
life as it used to be and as it shall be for evermore,
when the paper clips are pounded into penny whistles,
and the torn grey files into oratorios.

A FRAGRANT THOUGHT FOR TO-DAY

In this mad bad world where we live to-day,
Where sin like a panther stalks its prey,
And the demons of darkness about us throng
In the crowded streets as we walk along;
let us remember till journey's end
there's nothing so dear as the love of a friend.
    The helping hand as we climb the stile,
The cheery grin and the tender smile
Can cheer us along life's hard highway,
Whatever the cruel cynics say.
Since the world began true friends have found
'Tis love alone makes the world go round,
And so, of course, does a double rum
Thoughtlessly poured on an empty tum.

UPLIFT

Lift up your eyes
Unto the skies,
The parson said.

O weary one,
Sorrow is done,
Lift up your head.

Lift it up high,
Heaven is nigh,
Look, and you'll see . . .

Bombers, she said,
Fighters, she said,
And a doodle-bug coming for me.

'WE WHO HAVE HUSBANDS AT HOME . . .'

We who have husbands at home should be very quiet,
for we do not know
the meaning of days, nor yet do we understand
the hush of houses where in shadow go
the unheard footsteps, the invisible faces of men.
  Let us not speak
too loudly of war restrictions and rationing and the black-out,
for there are eyes that seek
empty horizons, skies and deserts, and sad grey seas,
and a sign from God,
while we who have husbands at home look in the shops
for wool perhaps, or cod.

Let us remember when we complain of the winter's cold,
there are others here
who have held in the moonless dark of a thousand nights
the hand of fear,
and have walked for years in desolate barren valleys
where no flowers grow.
    We who have husbands at home should be very quiet,
for we do not know.

COUNTRY HOTEL

Like driftwood tied neatly into bundles,
and stacked in little heaps beside the wall,
    the old ladies and gentlemen in the hotel
sit waiting for luncheon in the outer hall.

Though they have said everything a long time ago,
the white heads cluster together,
    to complain of the draughts and the lack of marmalade,
to remind one another of the weather.

The children circle round them gingerly,
knowing when not to speak and not to dance;
    quietly, quietly please, holding the white wool,
two plain, two purl for liberated France.

The major takes out his eyeglass and goes to the wireless.
The news! The news! From the first word to the last!
    Let the ear hear what the mind cannot fathom;
bombing and blood and blast.

Like elephants they stampede into the dining-room,
their pince-nezs jingle as they take their places.
    Put your bib on, darling Eric's child,
and don't pull silly faces.

    What? Is there pigeon for lunch again?
... We had a house once in a little street.
        ... We had a house once by the Sussex sea.
... We had a son once ... There's *blancmange* for sweet!

    Potter to the Post Office in the morning;
A little lie down after lunch on one's bed.
    And what will you do with your day, children?
The same as you, they said.

    The roots are torn up from the squares and gardens,
the branches are lopped off close to the tree;
    only the dead wood remains and the shoots
piercing a world they cannot see.

    Except for the good-looking woman in the corner,
who is either a duodenal or an international spy,
    the hotel is full of children waiting to live,
and old ladies and gentlemen waiting to die,

LOSING FACE

This is my doodle-bug face. Do you like it?
  It's supposed to look dreadfully brave.
Not jolly of course — that would hardly be tactful,
  But . . . well, sort of loving and grave.

You are meant to believe that I simply don't care
  And am filled with a knowledge supernal,
Oh, well . . . about spiritual things, don't you know,
  Such as man being frightfully eternal.

This is my doodle-bug voice. Can you hear it?
  It's thrillingly vibrant, yet calm.
If we weren't in the office, which *isn't* the place,
  I'd read you a suitable psalm.

This is my doodle-bug place. Can you see me?
  It's really amazingly snug
Lying under the desk with my doodle-bug face
  And my doodle-bug voice in the rug.

TO A FRISIAN COW

Geh Kuh! Überfreundlich Beast!
Bitte withdrawen Sie ein Schritt or two.
Du bist ein Bore zu sag the very least,
Du laut gebreather, tail beswitcher du!
Seh! Das Feld ist voll von Buttertassen,
Unter den Linden es gibt kuhle Shade;
Habe die Gütigkeit zu uns gelassen
Mit unser sandwiches und limonade.

SECOND SIGHT

They who had seen such beautiful things in their time,
The treasures of continents liberally laid before them —
Spring in the south of France, Florence in June,
The glories of Greece, the secrets of Egypt's tombs,
Kings in their coaches riding in proud processions,
Yachts floating white in rich blue tropic seas,
Peacocks on summer lawns by rose pink castles,
Court balls, cathedrals, Paris, and Samarkand —
They who had seen such beautiful things in their time,
Whose eyes had been ever blessed by loveliness,
Stood still, amazed, at the top of the Edgware Road,
And looked at the tiny trembling newborn lights
Casting their pitiful glow on the greasy streets,
Casting their small pale pools on the furtive kerb;
Stood still, in silence, speechless with adoration.
And their eyes, betrayed, were suddenly filled with tears,
Not having seen such beautiful things for a long time.

SPRING IN TOTHILL STREET

Spring comes slowly to Tothill Street.
   No banners. No bugle call.
Three daffodils in a milk jug,
   A shadow or two on the wall,

A shaft of sun in the passage
   To bless the Government green,
A lovelier light on the ink stains
   Where tired elbows lean.

The women who bend over blotters
    Can see with but inward eye
Their faraway homes and gardens,
    The leaf on the bough, the sky,

The cherry that blows in the orchard,
    The moss growing lush on the fell.
(There are typists with teeth typing Memos
    On the other side of the well.)

Mrs. Huxley may peer from her window
    For banks where bluebells spill,
She will find but a potted primrose
    On the Messenger's window-sill.

Miss Brassey who might be in Berkshire
    Miss Owen who should be in Wales,
Rest their ears on the telephones
    And listen to sombre tales

Instead of birdsong at morning,
    Or rill's song bubbling clean,
And lambs that have called to their mothers
    The long, long years between.

Spring comes slowly to Tothill Street.
    It passes, unnoticed, each day.
The daffodils in the milk jug
    Are dead. Throw them away.

ENTENTE CORDIALE

I am Mrs. St. John Blanding's secretary,
    and I write all her letters to Mrs. Dwight;
they are so long and so wonderful I have to
    take them home to finish them at night.

I like doing this, of course, but sometimes I wonder
    whether I couldn't come to an understanding
with Mrs. Dwight's secretary, who, I presume,
    writes all those wonderful letters to Mrs. St. John Blanding.

SEATS

Well, well, well! Here are the dear old faces
coming back to the dear old places
again. Now isn't that fun?
    Every one, yes, my dear, every one
is in London. Of course, it was an awful bore
but they simply could *not* get here before;
although they tried and tried,
they were tied
to the country houses they leased at such vast cost,
and they felt oh, so miserable and lost
away from their darling city.
    So we *must* have pity,
and let them have all the theatre seats,
and cinema seats,
and restaurant seats,
and taxi seats
(poor sweets!).
    After all, *we* had the fun of seeing London burn,
and now it's *their* turn.

THE VOICE OF THE WORLD

I am grateful for so many things,
said the old lady who had lost everything.
The warmth of the sun, the little flowers
make me so happy; and I like my wee chats
with the other old ladies in the hotel.
I can see the sea from my window too,
and I am doing a dear little piece of tapestry work.
God has been so good to me, and I glory each day
in the wonders of His creation.

    Aw, nuts! said the young man who had everything,
holding the sun, the sea, and the flowers in his hands.
The world is a lousy place and sick to the heart.
Glory? he said. Wonder? he said. Good night!

    But of course she was right.

IN 1945 IT WAS HANDED OVER . . .

They are scything the hay on the terraces,
  Next year the lawns will be smooth and green,
The thistles will be gone from the herbaceous borders,
  Everything will be clean.

The big house is opening its shuttered eyes;
  Ping go the blinds and a duster flaps.
The housemaid is not interested in history,
  Polishing up the taps.

Into the great ballroom came the Prince Regent,
  For his sake were all the candles lit;
Chase the dust of five years off the dining-room table,
  Spray the curtains with Flit.

Down the broad avenues walked the generations,
  The same fair English face coming home,
And still the pillars shine pink in the evening sunset
  And rosy glows the dome.

The voices of young men echo between the hedges,
  Soldiers, they died in a dozen wars.
Some one is putting bars up again in the nursery,
  And beeswax on the floors.

Soon the urns will be filled with cherry pie,
  (But this, this is the last carnation)
Oh fling open wide the doors for the lunatics sent
  By the Corporation.

1946

A THOUGHT FOR DENMAN STREET

Young man in a purple suit,
balanced on pointed ginger feet
at the corner of Denman Street,
selling illicit silk stockings
with fancy clockings
in the furtive half-light
of a dirty drunken Piccadilly night;

young man in a purple suit
doing a little business on the side,
it was not for you my son died.

   He died (not that you care)
because once, long ago, you were
kind to your mother,
and because at one time or another
you have spoken the truth.

   For Truth and Love he seemed, in his youth
to die,
but by and by
you will find, when you come to count the cost,
it is you we mourn, you who are lost,
young man in a purple suit.

I CAN HEAR MUSIC

I can hear music from a long way off.
Faint it is, but there are people stopping to listen,
pausing in the middle of their work to turn
their heads towards the unrecognizable tune.

   It is not much of a sound at the moment;
but everywhere, all over the world,
there are stiff hands stretching out to grope
for slack-stringed violins and tarnished trumpets,
for out-of-tune pianos and reedless bassoons.

   There is a snapping open of velvet cases,
and a whisking of green baize off the keys,
and a tinkle of rosin on to the parquet floor.
There is a moistening of lips grown dry with words of command,
and a trembling of fingers rigid from rifle's rim.

The voices are lifted again, uncertain, strange,
but coming towards us every day from the seas
and the desert lands, the dark lands where singing
has been muffled under the sad beat of the drums.
Soon we shall know the tune, and shall run to our doors
as the orchestras thunder by with bright bugles blowing,
to join in the song which though lost was never forgotten,
the heart, like an uncaged bird, winging to God.

THE TUMBRILS

They tell me the tumbrils are coming,
   The shafts are newly painted a bloody-red,
The horses are being hired from a brewer,
     So it is said.

People have already heard the creak
   Of the wheels, and the drivers' horrid cries,
And over the golden streets of Belgravia
     A vulture flies.

The drivers are practising with their whips,
   Lashing themselves into a fine frenzied state,
They are even teaching the horses' moustaches
     To curl with hate.

Somebody also met a woman
   Who had bought a tasselled cap of scarlet tweed;
That there has been a *lot* of knitting lately
     One must concede.

So we are for it! There is no hope.
   Death in a carriage-and-pair stands at the door.
We should be afraid if we hadn't been so
     Frightened before.

Nobody likes the sound of tumbrils,
  Yet we hope to greet ours with aplomb,
For it cannot possibly make as much noise
      As a V bomb.

Though the axles squeal like wild banshees,
  Though charged with black thunder are the horses' hoofs,
We also heard the sound of shrapnel falling
      On to the roofs.

As for the lady in the red cap,
  Dear old fire-watcher, dear old tea-drinker still,
What brave blitz stories we shall swop on the way
      To Tower Hill!

LOVE POEM

  When I am in the desert of a dinner-party,
or sitting on some tired smoke-wreathed committee,
or listening to a speech about the United Nations,
my thoughts run to you, my darling, as swiftly
as winged antelopes.
  In the noise and confusion I come to you who are quiet,
from the impermeable boredom of conversation
I turn to the sound of your voice,
and the horrible secret faces of strangers
merge into yours which I know and love so well.
  You will understand this, and yet when I tell you
that yesterday I was swept with a wild wave of love for you
standing beside a counter of pickled peaches
in Fortnum and Mason's,
you will not understand. Indeed, it was very surprising.

VJ DAY

Hurray! Hurray!
this is the day
when the whole nation
joins in the celebration
of everlasting peace;
so let me hit this policeman
as hard as I can.
    Whoopee
for liberty!
    Destruction is absolutely at an end,
so I will see if I can bend
this park chair.
    There!
    Now for goodness sake let's try and make it burn.
I yearn
I aspire
to have the world's most beautiful fire,
and it would really please
me if we could have it right under the trees,
so that at any rate, God willing,
I shall have done just a little bit of killing.
    Law and order is established throughout the world.
Look! I have hurled
the No Entry sign
into the Serpentine.
    Swept from the earth are the vandals.
I have broken off the door handles
of this car,
Ah! Ah! Ah!
over she goes, give her another shove;
peace, prosperity, and brotherly love.
    This is the day for which we fought and prayed.
Call out the Fire Brigade.

THE RELUCTANT SHEPHERDESS

She sits, the lady of my despair
by old, obstructive sheep
who stand in silent clumps and stare,
who look but do not leap.
She leans her crook upon the gate
through which her flock should clamber,
and settles down inanimate
to read Forever Amber.

Her collie, straying widdershins,
turns homeward to his kennel;
she has not seen the aspirins
nor heard of Alice Meynell.
Though moons may rise and stars may set,
she bars the road to sleep,
my shepherdess who will not let
me count her ruddy sheep.

IT IS LOVELY TO THINK . . .

It is lovely to think of all the young people
  who are going to reshape the world;
To massage its tired face in their strong hands,
  and get its hair curled.

Prancing with vigour they wheel at the starting-post;
  glossy and proud, beautiful and bright.
Waiting to turn ashes into flowers,
  and wrong into right.

Sweeping this way and that, their radiant sun-shot eyes
    cover the whole earth with plans of love.
Theirs the beauty of a young lion,
    the heart of a dove.

Theirs is the power, the glory, and the blue-print,
    the building, the land, the patterned life,
the good things: peace, security, laughter,
    for man and his wife.

And when they are old and their battered swords are sheathed,
    their torn and trailing banners stand furled,
it is lovely to think of their children
    reshaping the world.

THE LETTER

You cannot conceive, wrote the countess,
what conditions are like over here.
Everything, wrote the countess, is utterly depressing,
the future is unutterably drear.
    We've none of us any clothes you know;
I wear the same old dresses I wore
two years ago, and though I dare say they are adequate
they are such a *blistering* bore.
    We are caving in with the cold, wrote the countess,
and though all the fires are alight,
George and I have to go without baths if you please,
nearly every Saturday night,
and the central heating is very feeble,
and the gas heaters give out next to no heat,
and I simply won't break your heart, wrote the countess,
by telling you what we eat!

I know you cannot imagine, wrote the countess,
being so far away,
what terrible hardships we endured during the war years,
and are *still* enduring to-day.
    Where are the fruits of victory, I ask myself?
Have we won, my friend, only to lose?
Where is the nail varnish and the extra petrol coupons?
Where are the bananas and the shoes?
    Oh, I do wish I were dead, wrote the countess,
as dead as a slice of spam!

    I am thinking of you, answered Miss van der Byl,
writing from Rotterdam.

FOR THIS RELIEF...

Because your husband was killed in a concentration camp,
Because your brother was beaten until he died,
Because your friends have been taken away and tortured,
Because you have lost all faith, all hope, all desire,
Because there is nothing more in the whole wide world for you to lose,
I, full of compassion, send for your comfort,
Two of my husband's vests and a pair of old tennis shoes.

DINNER PARTY, 1946

The flushed faces are lit by candles on the table,
Cigar ash on the Worcester, scent on the sable,
'What are we arguing about?' 'How did it all start?'
'I hate you, I hate you from the bottom of my heart!'
'Silly young puppy!' 'What do *you* know of the Law?'
'Why not admit, dear, you've never read any of Shaw?'

'All small men, Tiny, tend to become bombastic,'
'It doesn't suit you, my lovely, to be quite so sarcastic.'
Pass the port round again, drop the napkins on the floor,
On all quietness and grace let us close the door,
Let us stick to our own opinions and shout down the others,
The something something sons and daughters of their mothers.
WheeEEE . . . goes the bus starting up from bottom into second,
And as though Death itself, with an alabaster hand, beckoned,
Silence falls. Foes look quickly into the eyes of friends,
Seeking with gentle glance to make amends,
While the quarrelling hearts rush lovingly to each other in fear . . .

Is it the end of the Warning or the start of the All Clear?

LE U.N.O. ET W.V.S.

Je parle du W.V.S., Madame Ystz.
Comment, madame?
Et bien, c'est une éspèce d'organisation de femmes.
Oui.
Si.
Et bien, madame, je pense
que since votre mari est tellement busy au Conference
vous n'avez probablement pas beaucoup a faire.
Je me make myself claire?
Et bien, nous serons enchantées de vous rendre
service, et si vous aimeriez, nous pouvons vous prendre
quelquepart pour voir quelquechose.
Le National Gallery peut être, ou Madame Tussaud's?
Où des jolies morçeaux d'Angleterre?
Où le East End bomber pendant la guerre?
N'importe où,
c'est up to you.

Et bien, c'est juste, madame, comme vous pensez.
Nous avons beaucoup de femmes, comme moi, qui parlent français,
et qui, comme vous,
n'avaient rien du tout
a faire.
    Oui, c'est extraordinaire,
mais je parle, vous voyez, du W.V.S., Madame Ystz.

A LULLABY IN POOR TASTE

(*To be sung in Westminster*)

Hushabye baby, a hush to your crying,
See how the gay little flags are a-flying,

Sleep without fear in your blanket of fleece,
Lullaby Java, rockaway Greece,

Doze in your blue-ribboned nest of inertia,
Pop go the Poles and pat-a-cake Persia.

Run to your dreams where the little lambs play,
Mr. Vishinsky has come for the day,

And nothing can harm you O infant most blest,
Ride a cock Palestine, peep-bo Trieste.

Lully my darling, till atom bombs fall,
When up will go baby and mummy and all.

THE MIRACLE

What is this strange, strange love that binds me
fast to the ink-stained desk, to the life not worth living?
Free am I, as a singing bird flying the skies,
  yet I stay on my little perch, songless and sad.
What is this thing that stops me running fleetfoot
to join the mink coats going into matinées;
to join the turban hats and the poodles on tartan leads
in a cup of hot chocolate served every morning in Bond Street?
Is it a love of habit or a love of duty?
Is it an easier task perhaps, to stay than to go?
Can it be all those old faces, now so ineffably boring,
and yet so beloved? Or an urge to be sacrificed?
Oh love is a strange thing, and who shall construe it:
but this, this is a love which is nigh to a miracle,
binding me tight to a life that is not worth the living,
free though I be, like a singing bird flying the skies.

NATIONAL SERVICE

England, you darling old thing,
For Pete's sake get quickly on to your feet again.
I am sick to death, dear heart, of working for you;
Come curls, come swiftly to your lion's mane!

I would fain lie myself down
On that terraced bosom of yours where the back slides.
Knowing your unicorn would not come to stab me
Home to the galleys where my conscience rides.

Buck up, England, my lovely!
I will give you one last long pull tho' break my heart,
One more spit and a polish to your golden crown;
Then, Mother, let your little one depart.